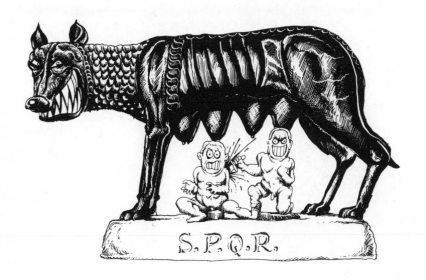

IMPERIAL
EXITS

JULIUS CICATRIX
AND MARTIN ROWSON

IMPERIAL EXITS

ST. MARTIN'S PRESS
NEW YORK

Library of Congress Cataloging-in-Publication Data

Cicatrix, Julius.
    Imperial exits / Julius Cicatrix and Martin Rowson.
      p.   cm.
    ISBN 0-312-14624-8
    1. Roman emperors—Death—Humor. 2. Rome—
History—30 B.C.–A.D. 476—Humor. 3. English wit
and humor. I. Rowson, Martin. II. Title.
DG274.C53   1996
937'.06—dc20   96-24854
                                     CIP

First published in Great Britain by Macmillan,
an imprint of Macmillan General Books

First U.S. Edition: December 1996

10 9 8 7 6 5 4 3 2 1

CONTENTS

CONTENTS

PREFACE

Being Emperor of Rome had its disadvantages. True, one had immense power, and although you may have had to fight the occasional war and sit through a few court cases you could hope to devote a good part of your life to ease and luxury. But for how long? And what would get you first? Scheming palace officials, the disgruntled soldiery, or a foreign invader? Or perhaps instead you would die a horrible death from natural causes, cursed by God for persecuting the Christians?

It was not an encouraging prospect, but there was never any shortage of candidates to become Roman Emperor, even during those troubled periods when emperors fell like ninepins.

In one respect Roman Emperors may have thought themselves singularly lucky, at least after death. For they used their power to have themselves declared gods by their successors. Unless a change of dynasty intervened, most Roman Emperors could expect to be deified in death, even if they had been hated in life.

The varied and often violent deaths of Roman Emperors are told in detail and with evident relish by ancient historians. This means that we frequently know more about an emperor's final hours than about any equivalent part of his life. It is the plan of the present offering to bring (with suitable illustration) a selection of these stories to life, retaining that mordant humour or gruesome gleefulness which infects the originals.

IMPERIAL
EXITS

JULIUS CAESAR
XLIV · BC

Any account of imperial Roman deaths must begin with the most famous of them all: the murder of Julius Caesar. Yet paradoxically Julius Caesar was by no means the first politician to be murdered at Rome, nor was he even an emperor. Emperors began only with his adopted son, Caesar Octavian (Augustus). But Caesar's death is, thanks to Shakespeare, the most memorable. We still remember the Ides of March, even if we've long ago forgotten what Ides means.*

Julius Caesar was both clever and ambitious, a talented general and an adroit politican – up to a point. His biggest political mistake was the one he didn't live to repeat. He fatally underestimated how much he was disliked by people he thought were his friends.

Having enlarged both the Roman empire and his own glory, he decided he would no longer brook any rivals and in 49 BC made the fatal crossing of the River Rubicon, saying as he did so 'alea iacta est' – the die is cast. This was a declaration of war

---

* Boringly enough, all it does mean is **the** fifteenth of the month.

– he had left his province and invaded Italy. Most of the senate, led by Pompey 'the Great', fled to Greece, where Caesar defeated them the following year. Pompey himself escaped to Egypt, where he was captured and killed by the reigning pharaoh. Caesar himself spent several years on mopping-up operations, entanglement with Cleopatra in Egypt, and victory in Africa and Spain.

This left him uncrowned king of Rome. But the Romans didn't much like kings. Not only did they have a republican constitution, which allowed their aristrocrats to run the government; they also had bad memories of the last king of Rome, Tarquin the Proud. They had thrown him out five centuries previously for indiscretions committed by his son. So when the crowds hailed Caesar as king, he cannily told them he was just plain Caesar. Only he didn't act as just plain Caesar.

In fact he became rather overbearing. He doled out consulships much as he pleased, and reformed the calendar – which needed doing, but still provoked resentment. Nor did the Romans believe Caesar when he said he didn't want to be king. They thought his refusal was just a clever ploy, and that he was testing the waters and waiting for the moment when public opinion was on his side.

This conviction gained strength at the Lupercalia, a bizarre annual festival when young men of good birth ran nearly naked through the city hitting women with goat-skin whips. It took place on February 15th, and Caesar presided over the whole affair seated on a golden throne. The day before, he had had himself made dictator for life. Then in the middle of the race one of the runners, Caesar's friend Mark Antony, ran up and

IV

AUGUSTUS

AD · XIV

The long reign of Augustus, the first official Roman emperor, was punctuated by the demise of friends and relations. The pattern was set early in life by the death of his real father, Gaius Octavius, when Augustus was only five years old. Gaius died suddenly while he was on his way back from a short spell governing Macedonia. Then, when he was nineteen, his uncle Julius (Caesar) gave Augustus his big chance, when in his will Julius adopted him as his heir. Not everyone was sure that a person could be adopted posthumously, but it happened anyway. Augustus became a rich and powerful nineteen-year-old, and set out to avenge his new-found father.

In order to do this he allied himself with Mark Antony, a man who had as few scruples as himself. After arguing with each other for a little while they joined forces and defeated Brutus and Cassius at Philippi in northern Greece.

That was in 42 BC. Augustus and Mark Antony then divided the Roman empire between them. Antony went east and got entangled with Cleopatra, the queen of Egypt famous for her nose. Augustus took charge of the west, including Italy

itself. He was preoccupied for a while with local rivals: stamping out the piratical Sextus Pompey, who had seized Sicily, and Marcus Lepidus, who had been given control of North Africa but decided the western provinces would do very nicely as well.

With Sextus Pompey and Lepidus removed only Antony and Cleopatra stood between Augustus and total power. That situation did not last long, since in 31 BC the pair were defeated by Augustus at the Battle of Actium. This led to another death in the family. Antony had married Octavia, Augustus's elder sister, in 40 BC, and so become Augustus's brother-in-law. He committed suicide the year after Actium.

Augustus then became sole ruler and was officially installed as the first Roman Emperor on 16 January 27 BC. That didn't stop his family dying, however.

The next important death came four years later: his nephew Marcellus. He was the son of Augustus's younger sister, who was being groomed as the emperor's successor since Augustus had no sons of his own. He even married Augustus's daughter, the beautiful but promiscuous Julia. Marcellus was only nineteen when he died, carried off by an illness that had nearly put paid to Augustus earlier that summer. Augustus had survived the illness through the ministrations of his doctor, an easterner called Antonius Musa. Encouraged back to health by cold baths and cold potions, Augustus recovered, but even cold baths and cold potions could not save Marcellus.

Did he fall, or was he pushed? Many Romans thought there was more to Marcellus's death than 'the character of that year and of the year following, which proved so unhealthful that great

X

numbers perished during them'. 'Cui bono?' they asked. And well they might, for an answer was easily to hand.

Here we must introduce a leading player in this gruesome tale: Augustus's formidable wife, Livia. As we said, she didn't give Augustus any sons, but she had already given two to her previous husband: Drusus and Tiberius. Why shouldn't they be Augustus's heirs? That is what eventually happened, but rumour had it she helped matters along by a judicious poisoning here and there, beginning with Marcellus.

The register of deaths continued with Marcus Agrippa, Augustus's closest friend, in 12 BC. He had married the lovely Julia after Marcellus's death, and they had had two sons, Gaius and Lucius, both of whom Augustus adopted as his heirs. Livia can't have been pleased, but they survived into their teens, a pair of pampered puppies, before succumbing to 'illness'.

Lucius died of 'illness' at Marseilles in AD 2 while on his way to Spain. Gaius, the elder, had meanwhile been sent to the east in 1 BC to deal with various problems, above all the troublesome Armenians. He was besieging an Armenian fortress when he allowed himself to be lured close to the walls by the wily commander and was wounded. The fortress was captured, but Gaius never recovered from the wound. He became depressed, resigned his command, and took ship for home. He got no further than Limyra in southern Turkey where he died of 'a sudden illness' in AD 3. A case of another 'unhealthful year', helped along by Livia.

Augustus himself followed ten years later. The first to know of it was apparently an eagle which flew round him and settled on the *A* of Agrippa on a statue base. Since Agrippa was dead this was considered bad news. Then lightning melted the *C* of Caesar on one of his statues, conveniently turning it into *aesar*, the Etruscan word for god. Augustus was clearly *en route* to divinity.

He was hurried on his way by the unfailing efforts of Livia. She had at last managed to have her son Tiberius recognized as heir, and wasn't going to give Augustus the chance for a late change of heart. When Augustus got a touch of diarrhoea, nobody thought anything save that here was an old man who needed a few days to recuperate. Neither they nor Augustus realized that Livia was daubing poison on figs from Augustus's own fruit trees. Figs are perhaps not the best thing to eat with loose bowels, still less so if they have been painted with poison. To disarm suspicion (so she thought) Livia carefully left some figs unpoisoned, so she could pick and eat them herself as if nothing were wrong.

Augustus died surrounded by his friends. He told them how he had found Rome clay and left it marble (a fact they may already have observed). Then he asked them to clap. He had been a hypocrite all his life (a ruthless power-seeker who had pretended to be the father of his people) and felt he deserved some applause. Fair enough. But Livia had played her part even better.

TIBERIUS
AD · XXXVII

Augustus was a man of charm and tact. Tiberius, on the other hand, was glum and stern. People couldn't make out whether he was really sinister or simply gauche, but either way he wasn't popular. Augustus was in any case a hard act to follow, but Tiberius didn't do himself any favours by shutting himself away with troops of young boys in his country villa. Nor by maltreating his relatives (though that soon became standard imperial procedure).

The relatives he took a special dislike to were his nephew's wife and her sons. His nephew was Germanicus, a popular fellow who died in mysterious circumstances in Syria during the early years of the reign. Germanicus left a widow, Agrippina, and a flourishing brood of six children, three sons and three daughters (not to mention three who had died in infancy). Now Tiberius had no children of his own, so all three of his great-nephews, plus Tiberius Gemellus, his sole surviving grandson, thought they had a chance of succeeding him as emperor. And that was where they went wrong.

The first to fall foul of Tiberius were Agrippina and her eldest son Nero (not to be confused with the famous Nero who did become emperor). They were arrested for treason in AD 29, declared enemies of the state, and sent into exile.

Agrippina ended up on Pandateria, a small island off the Italian coast. Being exiled didn't warm her feelings towards Tiberius, and he ordered a centurion to beat her up, which was carried out so thoroughly that it destroyed one of her eyes. Then she resolved to starve herself to death, but Tiberius had her force fed. When eventually she did die, he pointed out how lenient he had been in not having her strangled at once, but allowing her to live out her days on an island. The senate dutifully passed a decree commemorating this amazing act of clemency.

Nero was sent to another small Italian island called Pontia where, with a little encouragement, he conveniently killed himself.

That left two sons of Germanicus – but not for long. Drusus was accused of treason like Nero and his mother before him, and imprisoned in a cellar below the Palatine Hill at Rome. He survived there for two years, until his gaolers simply stopped feeding him, then hung on a further eight days by chewing the stuffing of his mattress.

While all this was going on Tiberius was living in retirement on Capri. Malicious gossip had it that he passed his time there debauching young boys and maidens: the rooms of his villa were painted with pornographic diagrams showing victims how they were to perform. Another of his amusements was to summon people to trial and when they were convicted have them thrown off the cliffs. In case that wasn't enough, he had boatloads of

soldiers stationed below to finish them off. He was also credited with an ingenious prank of tricking men into drinking large quantities of wine and then tying up their private parts.

This is what the Romans thought was going on at Capri. The reality was nearly as bad. Tiberius took to torturing people with his 'wit', coupling that with interesting questions on mythology such as 'Who was Hecuba's mother?' Such was the price of an imperial dinner invitation, and it was serious stuff. One grammarian had the bright idea to ask Tiberius's attendants in advance what the emperor was reading at the moment. He was banished for his impudence and later driven to suicide.

Tiberius had another special pleasure on Capri: rearing a viper for the Roman people. This was Caligula, the last of Agrippina's sons. He was eighteen when he went to live with the old man at his island retreat, and soon won Tiberius's affection by his own dissolute behaviour and proclivities. Partners in debauchery, Caligula was soon named Tiberius's heir and successor. The young man made his succession doubly sure by climbing into bed with Ennia Naevia, the wife of the praetorian commander Macro. One might have thought this was a bad way to win Macro's support, but the reality was the opposite, and when Tiberius fell ill early in 37, Macro was at Caligula's side.

Tiberius had left Capri for one of his customary perambulations of Campania. He already wasn't feeling too well when he went to see some games organized by the soliders. These 'games' included Tiberius throwing darts at a wild boar from his ringside seat, and by all accounts the exercise did neither boar nor emperor any good. The emperor got a pain in his side, and retired to his coastal villa at Misenum on the mainland opposite Capri. The boar, presumably, was past caring.

Tiberius tried to pretend he wasn't as ill as he seemed, and continued to hold banquets and feasts. But a wily physician managed to feel his pulse, and declared to Macro that the emperor wouldn't last above a couple of days. On March 16th his breathing seemed to have stopped. Caligula took the ring of office from his finger and went outside to be greeted as the new emperor by soldiers and attendants. Then all of a sudden news came that Tiberius had come round again and was calling for his dinner. There was nothing for it but to finish the job that nature had left half-done. Scarcely batting an eyelid, Macro went back to the imperial bedchamber and smothered the old man with a pillow. For this resolute action he was killed by Caligula the following year.

CALIGULA

AD · XLI

Being named after an army boot was not an auspicious start for a would-be emperor. Caligula's parents called him Gaius, but when he was with the Rhine army aged two his mother dressed him up as an infant soldier, booties and all. It is the nickname he is remembered by, though he took steps to punish anybody who used it to his face.

Neither was he blessed with a handsome appearance. He was tall and pale, with thin neck and legs, and though his head was bald his body was covered with hair. His enemies said he improved on his ugliness by practising terrifying expressions in a mirror. Yet he was also a devoted family man with a ready wit, and by no means an out-and-out monster.

Caligula's reputation didn't improve when he became emperor. He decided that a person of his standing should be revered as a god, and pretended to hold conversations with Jupiter. At a wedding reception he took a fancy to the bride and married the lady himself, only to divorce her a few days later. He was also rather fond of chariot racing, and built his own private stadium at the Vatican.

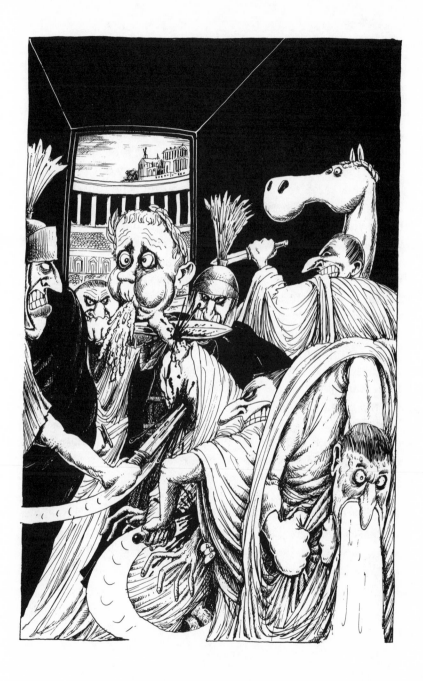

To pull his chariots he had top-notch racehorses. The one we hear most about was Incitatus, 'Speedy', who had an ivory manger, purple blankets, and a jewelled collar. The poor animal was sometimes taken to dinner and offered golden barley to eat. Caligula eventually hit upon the bright idea of making him consul, though it was a joke he didn't live to carry out.

Caligula came to power amid general rejoicing on 18 March AD 37. Dour old Tiberius was dead, and here in his place was a bright young thing keen on holding games and parties. Just three years later Caligula had become thoroughly unpopular with the senators (many of them executed for their part in conspiracies, real or imagined), and even with his own household. He may not have slept with all his sisters, but he certainly banished two of them to a small rocky island. His final mistake was to antagonize the praetorian guard.

The conspiracy which formed against Caligula was so wide-ranging it was almost bound to succeed. It included Clemens, the commander of the praetorian guard, and Callistus, one of the top men in the palace administration. These powerful people kept themselves at a distance, and encouraged others to do the dirty work. But even so, the plot nearly came to grief late in AD 40 when one of the conspirators was arrested. To save his life this man named a whole string of accomplices, but as luck would have it he tagged on the name of the emperor's wife, Caesonia. Caligula couldn't believe she was involved, decided the whole thing was a pack of lies, and had the man killed anyway.

By January 41 the assassins were ready. The leading roles in the killing itself were to be taken by officers of the praetorian guard, who had daily access to Caligula and would naturally go about armed. One of the officers, Cassius Chaerea, had particular reason to hate the emperor. He was a brave man, and some years before had cut his way through a mutinous army single-handed: but he had the misfortune of a high-pitched voice and Caligula, ever the one for a laugh at somebody else's expense, had taken to calling him 'lassie'.

Chaerea and his fellow officer Cornelius Sabinus decided to make their attempt on January 24th, when Caligula would be watching the Palatine Games. These games, lasting several days, were held every year in a temporary wooden theatre built on top of the Palatine Hill, next to the imperial palace.

Caligula spent the morning of the 24th enjoying himself, having fruit tipped down on to the spectators and watching the squabbles that broke out. He was blissfully unaware that most of the senators sitting around him were waiting for him to be killed. He usually left the theatre around midday for a bath and lunch in the palace, before returning to the games for the afternoon session. Chaerea had decided the best place to kill him would be in the narrow passage leading from the theatre to the palace, where no one could come to his rescue. As luck would have it, Caligula didn't much feel like lunch on this particular day, since his stomach was upset from over-indulgence the night before. It looked as if Chaerea would have to kill him where he sat, without any hope of escaping. Then all of a sudden there was a commotion as Caligula and his entourage at last left their seats and walked out of the theatre.

First to emerge were Claudius (the future emperor) and Marcus Vinicius, Caligula's brother-in-law. They went back to the palace by the main route, but Caligula turned aside into a narrow passage where some Asiatic boys were rehearsing a hymn composed in his honour. While he was speaking to them, Chaerea went up and requested the password for the day. As Caligula turned, Chaerea drew his sword and hacked into his neck, shouting 'Take that!' The blow wasn't fatal, however, since it was stopped by the collar bone, and Caligula dashed forward to escape. He didn't get far, since he was tripped by Sabinus and pushed to the ground. Caligula writhed and shouted that he was still alive, but the other conspirators closed in and finished him off. Several of them stabbed him in the privates, and some in their hatred were alleged to have 'tasted of his flesh'.

The body lay covered in thirty wounds when the imperial litter-bearers burst upon the scene, brandishing their poles. They were followed by the fierce German bodyguards, but by this time the assassins had made themselves scarce. They didn't forget, however, to send Julius Lupus into the palace to kill Caesonia and splatter her daughter's brains across the wall.

The death of Caligula led some foolish souls to suppose that Rome would no longer be ruled by emperors but by the senate, as it had been until Augustus. The praetorian guard soon scotched that plan by seizing Claudius and declaring him emperor, since if there were no emperor, they would all be out of a job. Claudius arrested Chaerea and Lupus, and had them executed. For some reason Sabinus escaped conviction, but took his own life soon afterwards.

The assassins thus came to a deservedly violent end. Caligula's body meanwhile had been taken from the Palatine to the imperial gardens in the east of the city, where it was hurriedly cremated. It wasn't a particularly successful job, and when

Caligula's sisters returned to Rome a few months later they dug up the half-burned remains and cremated them again. But even that didn't finish him off; Caligula's troubled ghost was still making appearances on the Palatine many years later.

CLAUDIUS
AD · LIV

The emperor Claudius came to power by accident, when the guards found him hiding behind a curtain. He reigned for fourteen long years, and showed that by this time even a cripple with a stammer could frighten the Romans into obeying him. With the exception, that is, of his own women folk, who spent most of the reign serving their own pleasures and ambitions.

The first of these scheming women was Messalina, a pretty young girl of fourteen when the forty-eight-year old Claudius married her in AD 40. They had two children, but Messalina soon showed her interests extended beyond family life to various other men. She persuaded Claudius to have her own enemies killed, but then went too far by marrying one of her admirers, Gaius Silius. It wasn't a winning strategy, to divorce a husband who was also the emperor, and Messalina was executed for her intrigues.

Claudius declared that enough was enough, that marriage was not for him, and that if he broke his word the praetorian guard had every right to kill him. A year later he married his niece Agrippina.

Agrippina had two unpleasant characteristics. The first was her own lust for power. The second was Nero, her son by an earlier marriage. Claudius got the son with the mother, though he waited a couple of years before formally adopting him as his heir.

By this time Claudius was an old man, at least by Roman standards. It was surprising he had survived so long, given the abrupt end meted out to his predecessor. It was even more surprising since Claudius was hardly the ideal man for the part, either physically or mentally.

Physically he was majestic and dignified – but only when he sat down and didn't speak. When he walked his weak knees gave him an ungainly gait. When he talked he stammered. And when he became angry or upset, he drooled from the nose and foamed at the mouth.

In public speeches he was rambling and inept. He interrupted a senate debate on butchers and vintners with the observation, 'Now, pray, who could live without a snack?' He was much given to feeble jokes, even when he was sitting in judgement on important law-suits. And he shared the fruits of his 'wisdom' even with the common people, issuing proclamations with snippets of such homely advice as 'Nothing is so effective a cure for snake-bites as the juice of the yew tree.'

Even yew juice proved ineffective against Nero and Agrippina.

Emperors were always the target of conspiracies, and Claudius was no exception. The first major danger had come in 42, when the governor of Dalmatia had risen in rebellion, backed by friends in Rome. The rising was quickly suppressed, and killing lots of Romans (whether they had been involved or not) helped to spread a kind of respect for the new regime.

The next year Claudius became an unlikely military hero by conquering Britain, a soft and rather pointless target. His great helpers were his court officials Pallas, Callistus, and Narcissus. These were freedmen (former slaves) who effectively ran the business of government on Claudius's behalf. All three stood to lose from Messalina's success, and worked together to thwart her. It was a different story when Claudius decided to remarry, since they each backed a different candidate. There were three ladies in the reckoning: the immensely wealthy Lollia Paulina, who had been wife to the infamous Caligula (for a very short time); Aelia Paetina, one of Claudius's own earlier wives (he was married altogether four times); and Agrippina, his niece, Caligula's sole surviving sister.

As we have seen, it was Agrippina who won this particular contest, backed by Pallas. Now from this point on the story becomes confused. It may be that Agrippina and her son Nero were models of decorum, that Claudius fell ill and died, and that Nero proved an exemplary ruler – for a few years, at least. But it is more interesting to believe the colourful tale of intrigue and murder which the Roman historians tell us.

The first scandalous element was the nature of relations between Agrippina and Pallas; not exactly platonic, we are told. Next were Agrippina's schemes to make sure that Nero was appointed Claudius's successor. This meant overturning the claims of Claudius's own son Tiberius Claudius Germanicus, who since the conquest of Britain had been known as Britannicus. The crucial step was taken in AD 50 when Claudius adopted Nero, and backed up when Nero married Claudius's daughter two years later. Britannicus's prospects looked black indeed.

The final stage was masterminded by Agrippina. With Nero's succession beyond question, all she had to do was to get rid of Claudius. Then she could rule in her son's name.

Her big opportunity came when Narcissus, her great enemy, fell ill and left Rome to convalesce at the seaside. With this last barrier removed Agrippina lost no time in recruiting the services of an expert poisoner, a woman named Locusta. Locusta supplied the poison and Halotus (the imperial taster) slipped it into Claudius's food.

The food in question was an extraordinarily fine mushroom. But there was a hitch; rather than dying, Claudius got a fit of the runs, and his poisoners began to think they had failed. Agrippina was a lady of resource, however, and at once called in the imperial doctor Xenophon. His instructions were to kill rather than cure his imperial patient. So while Claudius was retching and trying to vomit, Xenophon helped by sticking a feather in his throat. Only the feather had been dipped in a quick-acting poison.

After a night of torment, Claudius died, and at midday the following day, Nero was proclaimed emperor. They gave out that Claudius had died a natural death, and one of Nero's first acts was to have him proclaimed a god. So was the mushroom assured a place in history.

NERO

AD · LXVIII

The emperor Nero was a man of artistic sensibilities mixed with extraordinary cruelty. Not to be outdone by Caligula, he killed his mother as well as his wife, along with his stepbrother, sundry members of the senate, and anyone else who offended him. Nero coupled this with hypocrisy, declaring on one occasion, when asked to sign a man's death warrant, how he wished he had never learned to write. His teacher was Seneca, a Spanish stoic (one of those philosophers who believed in suffering in the face of human adversity). The variation adopted by Nero was that Seneca believed that the suffering should be done by oneself, while Nero transferred the experience to others.

Nero's big weakness was that he was more interested in musical battles than real ones. Not that there wasn't the odd victory during his reign: one of his generals drove the revolting Boudicca to powdered glass, while another thrashed the troublesome Armenians. But these weren't really victories for which Nero (at Rome) could claim much credit.

Nero's family life was troubled first by his mother and then by his wives. His mother Agrippina was in fact one of that dubious brood, the sister and brothers of Caligula. She had wormed her way into the affections of the elderly Claudius, until at last he had married her and adopted Nero as his son and heir.

When Nero became emperor he was only sixteen and Agrippina expected to rule the roost. But Nero soon grew tired of his mother and decided the time had come to dispose of her. He tried several methods without success: administering poison (she took antidotes); making the ceiling of her bedchamber collapsible so that she would be killed while she slept (the plan was leaked); and finally luring her to a banquet on the Bay of Naples, and sending her home in a specially sabotaged ship. The idea was that the canopy above her couch (which was heavily weighted) would fall on her and continue through the bottom of the boat. In the event the canopy missed her when it fell, and she jumped overboard and swam ashore to her villa. When he heard the news Nero decided to stop pretending and sent soldiers to execute her. But he was hounded by his mother's ghost ever after.

Compared to killing his mother, killing a wife or two came relatively easy. The first one, Claudius's daughter Octavia, was banished to a small island and murdered shortly afterwards. He then married Poppaea Sabina, one of the beauties of the age, but she came a cropper when she criticized Nero for coming home late from the races. He kicked her to death in a rage, even though she was pregnant.

His overthrow came in AD 68, and was a curious mix of domestic conspiracy and provincial revolt. The revolt was led by one Julius Vindex, governor of Gaul. Vindex's local levies were easily squashed by the mighty Rhine army, however, and for a

moment it looked as if Nero had won. But if the Rhine legions didn't like Vindex (a Gallic upstart) they weren't too keen on Nero either. And in fact Galba, governor of Spain, had already been proclaimed emperor instead.

Nero hung on at Rome, hoping the trouble would pass, but Galba's agents got to work on his officials, and Nero's cruelty and extortion came home to roost. The crux came when Galba's people managed to win over Nymphidius Sabinus, commander of the praetorian guard.

To escape certain death Nero decided to leg it, went to Ostia (the port of Rome), and tried to take ship for the east. But nobody would go with him, so he gave up the idea and went back to the palace. When he awoke there around midnight he found that his guards and attendants had gone, taking even the box of poison he had acquired in case of extremity. So he went out into the street, looking for somebody who would help him to commit suicide.

There he met one of his old palace officials, a man Phaon (pronounced 'Fon') who promised to help Nero escape from Rome. The two of them travelled in disguise to Phaon's villa just outside the city, making their way through the undergrowth and in by the back door. Once inside, Phaeon showed his true colours, urging Nero to kill himself there and then. So Nero ordered a grave to be dug, and with the words 'What an artist dies in me!' plunged a dagger into his neck. As he did so, a centurion rushed into the room to arrest him, but all the dying Nero could say was 'Too late' and 'This is fidelity.'

GALBA, OTHO, AND VITELLIUS

AD · LXIX

Nero's revenge was sharp, though he wasn't around to see it. Galba, the man who replaced him as emperor, was a wrinkled-faced senior citizen, seventy years old. People thought he was a bit of a martinet, and he was certainly old fashioned in most things, though he was an innovator in one: the first man at Rome to make elephants walk a tightrope (for the amusement of the populace, of course). When it came to walking the tightrope himself – the political tightrope between rewarding his followers or keeping them under control – he was less sure footed.

One of his key supporters was a much younger man, Marcus Salvius Otho. Now Otho had been one of Nero's closest friends – not in itself a reassuring commendation – and had got entangled with one of the greatest beauties of the time, Poppaea Sabina. Roman historians tell the story in different ways. The most scandalous version is that Nero wanted Poppaea for himself, but couldn't risk divorcing his own existing wife at the time. So he asked Otho to take charge of Poppaea; which he did – only rather too well! Otho was sent for his pains to the far ends of the earth (modern Portugal). There he met Galba, his next-door neighbour, the governor of Spain.

When Nero died, Galba and Otho set out together for Rome. Otho's great hope was that Galba would die (an Ancient Roman wasn't expected to live much past seventy) and that Otho would be named as his heir. But in order to make doubly sure of his prospects, he began to inveigle himself into the good graces of the imperial guard, and everyone else who might help him. He gave them gifts, while all they got from Galba was the sharp side of his tongue. But when Galba chose another man as his heir, Otho soon rallied the guards to his cause. When Galba came down to the Forum, he was confronted by Otho's guards, and an ugly scene erupted. The soldiers began by using Galba's litter (with him still in it) for target practice; and when (to their annoyance) they missed, they tumbled him out and finished the job with their swords. Galba's dying words were brave though futile: 'Do your work, if this is better for the Roman people.' Thus he died, killed by Camurius (or Terentius, or Lecanius, or Fabius Fabulus: the sources become confused at this point).

The soldiers chopped off Galba's head and stuck it on a spear, then whirling it aloft carried it to Otho. Then they sold it to the servants of Patrobius, a man Galba had had executed, who abused it some more. The head was finally rescued by Galba's steward, and buried with the body in the emperor's garden.

Galba was murdered on 15 January 69, after reigning six months. Otho didn't even manage that. Having disposed of Galba, he opened negotiations with Vitellius, hoping to avoid

war. But Vitellius had eight legions at his back, and wasn't to be bought off so easily. He didn't rush to do battle himself, but sent his generals on ahead to invade Italy. By April they had arrived at Cremona, and it was there that Otho with his smaller army decided to fight. Otho himself withdrew a few miles behind the lines to Brixellum to await the outcome. The First Battle of Cremona was fought on April 14th, and gave the Vitellians a complete victory; forty thousand men (mainly on Otho's side) were killed.

Otho nobly decided he had had enough, and chose his own way out. He remembered no doubt what his own soldiers had done to Galba. So he made a short speech, told his supporters to flee to safety by what means they could, then withdrew into his room. He spent a little time testing which of his two swords was the sharper, then put one beneath his pillow. Now here is the incredible part of the story: he dismissed his servants and went to sleep, so heavily that his personal attendants heard his snores! When he woke up next morning he took the sharper sword and fell on it, emitting just a single groan as he died.

Vitellius had a much less respectable end. After Otho's death he went on to Rome, where he was emperor throughout the summer and autumn of 69. In August, however, he found the tables turned when the forces of a new would-be emperor, Vespasian, invaded Italy. Vitellius sent his army north to deal with them, and as luck would have it the battle was fought on exactly the same ground as the earlier one against Otho: just outside Cremona. But whereas Vitellius had won the First Battle of Cremona it was Vespasian who won the Second.

In December 69 the victorious army arrived at Rome, where

Vitellius was still living in the imperial palace. When the soldiers broke into the city, he rather feebly tried to flee, but then gave up the idea and returned to the palace. He found it echoing and deserted, but tied a belt full of gold coins round his waist and sought a hiding place. The room he chose is variously described as a door-keeper's lodge or a kennel. Disguising himself in dirty old clothes, he tied a guard dog in front of the door and shoved a bed and mattress against it.

A closed door with a guard dog before it was hardly designed to divert suspicion, and the attacking soldiers soon broke it down. They dragged Vitellius out, covered in rubbish and blood (we are told the dogs had had a go at him), but *he* refused to tell *them* who he was, and *they* didn't recognize *him*. Not at first. Then the penny dropped, and without waiting for further orders the soldiers put a noose round his neck, pulled off his tunic, tied his hands behind his back, and dragged him into the Forum. The wretched man was pushed and punched all the way up the Sacred Way, mocked by the crowd for his protruding belly, and pelted with dung. When they arrived at the stairs leading up to the Capitol (the so-called Stairs of Wailing, where criminals' bodies were thrown) the soldiers indulged themselves in a bit of torture, then cut off Vitellius's head and threw the remains of the body into the Tiber.

XXXVII

VESPASIAN

AD · LXXIX

Vespasian was a man of wit and enterprise. He had the big advantage over most of his predecessors that he hadn't been brought up a pampered member of the imperial family, ever on the look-out for poison and intrigue, but was just an ordinary Roman. An ordinary, rather wealthy Roman, whose father had run a successful tax-collecting business in Switzerland. The gnomes of Zurich hadn't yet made their appearance, and Switzerland was hardly the financial centre of the Roman world, but his father evidently turned in a tidy profit.

It didn't do to look back much further; for envious tongues wagged that Vespasian's great-grandfather was not really a respectable citizen, since he came from (horror of horrors) northern Italy north of the Po. In Roman terms this was like saying you came from Doncaster; nothing wrong with it in itself, but hardly a place usually associated with the fashionable élite.

Vespasian's early life wasn't all that successful. It was only his mother's sarcasm that drove him into the senate. His first mentions there were for toadying to Caligula. Then he married a lady of such dubious background that she had to go to court

to prove she really was a Roman citizen. Most Romans found governing Africa was a gold mine, but when Vespasian was given the chance he made hardly any profit, his main claim to fame being pelted with turnips in the market at Hadrumetum.

He did rather better as a soldier, fighting the uncouth natives of southern and western Britain.

We first begin to warm to Vespasian when we read of his time in Greece. He went there in Nero's entourage, and in that capacity was expected to sit through the interminable imperial performances in all the main cities they passed through. The theatre exits were closed and nobody was allowed to leave till Nero was finished. People feigned death in order to be carried out and escape; women gave birth in the aisles. Vespasian simply fell asleep.

That did his standing with Nero no good at all, but he was still respected enough to be sent as commander-in-chief against the rebellious Jews. By the time that war was over, Nero was dead, Galba, Otho, and Vitellius were dead too, and Vespasian himself had become emperor.

He reigned for ten years in a calmly competent manner, leaving the dirty work of government to his portly son Titus. He amused himself with his concubines and his jokes, and with squeezing money out of his subjects. He was especially good at quoting poetry 'with great timeliness', saying for instance of a man with large private parts that he was 'Striding along and waving a lance that casts a long shadow' (a line taken from the *Iliad*). When a colossal statue was voted to him at public expense he was delighted, holding out his hand for the money and saying, 'The base is already here.'

XL

Vespasian took a nap every day before dinner and spent his summer holidays at Aquae Cutiliae, a spa town close to his birthplace. It was here too that he met his end. Sculptors and others had noticed that Vespasian went round with brows knotted in thought, as if he was racked by constipation. Had that been a problem earlier, it certainly didn't trouble his final days, since he went down with diarrhoea in the summer of 79. He struggled on with the business of government, but was forced to take to his bed. A stubborn old man, he held that an emperor ought to die on his feet. It was the runs that carried him off. Trying to stand again after a particularly fluid attack he collapsed and died in the arms of his attendants, saying, 'Oh dear! I think I'm becoming a god!'

TITUS

AD · LXXXI

Titus was insufferably bad before he became emperor and insufferably good afterwards. He was the eldest son of Vespasian, but was born long before his father came to power. During his insufferably good phase everyone wanted to make out what a distinguished childhood he had had and so invented a story that he had been a close friend of Claudius's son Britannicus. When Britannicus had drunk the poison, they said that Titus had finished off the last few drops, and was ill for a long time afterwards. Whatever the truth of the matter, it didn't stop him becoming a plump and rounded individual in later life.

As it happened, Titus's later life had barely got under way when he died. To tell the story properly, however, we need to go back to his father's reign. Titus was appointed commander of the praetorian guard by Vespasian and soon won a reputation for ruthlessness. He showed special promise as a forger, and managed to rid himself of several dangerous opponents by this creative writing.

When he became emperor on his father's death, he turned over a new leaf and got somebody else to his dirty work, just as

he had done Vespasian's. He was much given to hypocritical utterances, as when at dinner one evening he remembered he hadn't done anything for anybody that day: 'Friends,' he said, 'I have lost a day!'

Titus reigned for only two years, but these years saw two of the most famous events of Roman history. The first was the eruption of Vesuvius, and the smothering of Pompeii and Herculaneum by a huge fallout of ash. The second event was little less destructive of life and limb: the dedication of the Colosseum, the vast amphitheatre which Vespasian had begun. Wild beasts and gladiators fought for a hundred days to make sure the place was properly broken in.

Death came to Titus suddenly and unawares. He had just finished watching another bloodbath at the games and was travelling to his summer retreat in the hills when a peal of thunder broke from a clear blue sky. This was an awful omen, and Titus soon fell ill with a fever. Maybe it was a touch of malaria. Feeling worse and worse, he arrived at the country villa where Vespasian had died.

Enter Titus's younger brother Domitian, a man with an eye to the main chance. Titus was childless, which left Domitian next in line. The fever made him uncomfortably hot, so Domitian hit upon the idea of putting him in a box packed with snow (the Roman equivalent of a chest freezer?) to cool him down. The treatment worked to perfection – at least from Domitian's perspective. Titus quickly died.

DOMITIAN
AD · XCVI

Titus Flavius Domitianus (Domitian) was one of the less pleasant emperors to rule Rome. He was said to have loved nobody, except a few women, and to have introduced new forms of torture, such as burning rods in the privates, for those who conspired against him. Domitian was also a very fearful man, imagining assassins round every corner, a feature which made him even more dangerous to his associates. He built himself a huge new palace on the Palatine, and had some of the corridors faced with highly polished marble so that when he was strolling along them he could see who was behind him. Paranoia was the keyword. Domitian's private garden is still visitable, hidden away among tall palace buildings, and laid out with ornamental scalloped fountains and flower-beds.

Domitian wasn't averse to sexual licence in himself. People even said he put his wife away and cohabited with his niece, then in a *ménage à trois* when his wife was recalled. At the same time he could be a bit of a stickler on sex for others. One such instance was the case of the Vestal Virgins. These were six ladies who lived in a house in the Forum and tended the sacred fire in the Temple of Vesta. Evidently temptation had got the better of them and they had been acting less virginally than was prescribed. But while Domitian's predecessors had turned a blind eye to their indiscretions, Domitian had the unchaste virgins killed, even the Chief Vestal, who was buried alive.

Domitian's fear of assassination turned more and more to tyranny in his later years, and lots of senators were killed on flimsy charges of treason. His idea of clemency was to allow the accused to choose the kind of death they preferred. He also became puffed up with pomposity, renaming the month September 'Germanicus' in honour of his German victories and October 'Domitianus' after his birthday.

At last even his personal attendants had had enough, and decided to kill Domitian before Domitian killed them. Stephanus, steward to one of his family, offered to do the deed. He went round for several days with a dagger in his sleeve, concealed beneath a wrapping of bandages, saying all the time that he had just injured his arm. In order to succeed, he had to get Domitian alone, aside from his guards and other attendants, and to do this he drew up a false document containing some truly startling allegations of treason.

Domitian agreed to a private conference with Stephanus in the imperial bedchamber, with only a single boy servant in attendance. As soon as they were inside, the other conspirators locked the doors behind them. Then Stephanus handed over the paper and while Domitian was standing stock-still in amazement, Stephanus stabbed him in the groin. Why he chose the groin nobody explains, since it wasn't a very good spot for a quick and instant result. Domitian cried out to his boy to fetch the dagger

he kept under his pillow, and grappled Stephanus to the floor. The boy found nothing but the hilt – the blade had been removed by the conspirators as a precaution – and while Domitian was trying to gouge Stephanus's eyes out on the floor, the other assassins broke into the room and finished him off.

But the final indignity was still to come: the emperor's body was cremated by a nurse called Phyllis.

NERVA

AD · XCVIII

The emperor Nerva was another oldie, sixty-five when he came to power and sixty-seven when he died sixteen months later. He was a surprise choice to succeed Domitian – a safe pair of hands, perhaps, that weren't expected to live too long. But though he was an elderly senator, that didn't make him an altogether estimable character. He was credited with having debauched Domitian when the latter was a boy. That may have been idle street gossip. But he maintained his liking for young boys into later life.

People liked Nerva because he was a welcome change after Domitian. They pointed out how well he ruled, even forbidding men from castrating each other or marrying their nieces. But not everybody was satisfied. One person remarked that it was worse than under Domitian, since under Domitian nothing had been allowed, whereas under Nerva anything went.

The soldiery were even less impressed. How on earth did they end up with this sexagenarian emperor, ailing and weak? Hardly a commander they could respect, and not a man likely to lead them to glorious victories. He hadn't even punished the murder-

ers of their idol Domitian. Now there had been a man who had rewarded them handsomely for their loyalty.

The leader of the malcontents was Casperius Aelianus, commander of the praetorian guard. With a band of accomplices he burst into the palace and held the ageing Nerva at knife point, demanding the surrender of Domitian's killers. In a fit of tragic heroism Nerva bared his throat to his attackers – but surrendered the murderers just the same.

What happened next is an enigma. For Nerva, childless himself, decided to adopt a successor who would put a bit of backbone into his regime. But the man he adopted was someone he hardly knew. He might almost as well have picked the name out of a hat: Marcus Ulpius Traianus (the future emperor Trajan). Trajan had one major advantage on his side: he was Governor of Upper Germany, with a force of four legions at his disposal. We can't help suspecting that Trajan put his own name forward, an offer that Nerva could hardly refuse.

The adoption ceremony was in October 97. Three months later Nerva died. He was shouting angrily at one Regulus (the reason isn't recorded) when he started to sweat, then to shiver, and finally expired. It was a noisy rather than a dignified end.

HADRIAN
AD · CXXXVIII

The emperor Hadrian was a man of many parts. On the one hand he was a military commander who fortified the frontiers of the Roman empire with devices like Hadrian's Wall. On the other, he was an aesthete with pretensions to be something of a scholar. He was no cuddly philosopher, however, but a stern and cruel ruler who was so hated for the number of senators he had killed that those who survived nearly refused to make him a god.

Hadrian spent a lot of his reign travelling around his vast empire, checking up on officials and visiting the local beauty spots like a tourist. He particularly liked Athens, where he could indulge his love of all things Greek.

His family life was not a success, perhaps because he wasn't keen on women. One of the saddest events of his reign was the death of his (male) favourite Antinous, while they were sailing up the Nile. In Hadrian's autobiography (now lost) he said that Antinous had simply fallen overboard, but dark rumours circulated that he had been offered in sacrifice to further one of the emperor's schemes.

Hadrian was never more insufferable than when showing off

MARCUS AURELIUS
AD · CLXXX

Marcus Aurelius does not come over in his own writings (the famous *Meditations*) as a man who would have been good company at a party. He was the sort of person who would go to the Colosseum to see the games out of a sense of duty, but would take an improving book to read while he was there. In fact, he didn't much like bloodshed, and preferred the gladiators to fight with blunted weapons. It was rather bad luck, then, that he had to spend most of his reign fighting barbarians.

The Romans thought very highly of Marcus. He was the ideal emperor: firm, courteous, civilized, generous, and nobody's fool. Except perhaps his wife's – she spent a lot of her time on the coast of Campania (south of Rome) where she haunted the ports and harbours looking for sailors, because (it was said) they worked in the nude. Nor was his son Commodus a joy and support to him.

Marcus had other problems to contend with alongside his wife and son. For the first eight years of his reign he had to co-operate with his stepbrother, Lucius Verus. It probably came as a relief when Lucius died of an apoplexy.

There was also the plague which struck Rome in 166, and killed thousands of people in the capital and the major cities of Italy. Then there were the barbarian invaders who crossed the Danube and the Alps to invade northern Italy.

Finally Marcus Aurelius had to cope with the rebellion of one of his most trusted lieutenants, Avidius Cassius. Cassius was not a bad man, but he heard that Marcus was dead and was afraid that the empire would be bestowed on somebody other than Commodus, the rightful heir. (Here was a man who actually *wanted* Commodus to be emperor.) Unfortunately, Marcus wasn't dead, and Cassius was left in the unenviable position of finding he had rebelled by mistake. He was soon disposed of by one of the soldiers.

His dislike of bloodshed didn't stop Marcus from planning to conquer the whole of central Europe, and this was what he was doing when he died. His death was as dignified as his life, though by the end he had become a junkie. In his younger days he had been as keen as anyone on striking down wild boars from horseback, but his gathering illness made him too weak for such pursuits. It affected his stomach and chest and to alleviate the symptoms he took regular doses of opium. The drug, we are told, 'enabled him to endure both this and other maladies'. Not surprising that Marcus complained of the difficulty in dragging himself out of bed in the morning. The end came when for five days he refused to eat, and then on the sixth called his friends and advisers to his bedside and asked, 'Why do you weep for me, instead of thinking about the pestilence and about death which is the common lot of all of us?' The next day, he saw only his son, and he died in his sleep the following night.

COMMODUS

AD · CXCII

The emperor Commodus suffered the supreme indignity of being strangled by an athlete called Narcissus. This brought an untimely end to the imperial command performances when all top Romans were expected to flock to the amphitheatre to see their beloved ruler spearing a few elephants or shooting the head off the occasional ostrich. Going to the games was like going to the cinema today – oodles of blood and violence, but all at a safe distance. Famous gladiators became sex-objects, and had women swooning in their seats, but they weren't quite the thing for polite society. What scandalized the Romans even more was that Commodus didn't only attend the games – he actually took part in them. Seven hundred and thirty-five times.

It was good business, since he made a million sesterces every time he performed. But it wasn't much fun for his opponents, since he won with amazing consistency. He was especially good at slaying net-men (not to mention ostriches).

His big problem was megalomania. The reign began in a quiet kind of way. Commodus had little interest in government, so he employed able ministers to do the work instead. First there was

Saoterus, then Perennis, then Cleander, but all of them came to violent ends. So nearly did Commodus himself. One assassin had a go at him as he was leaving the amphitheatre, but stopped to explain his motives and was captured by the guard. In reply, Commodus made away with his wife and sister and withdrew from public life to the comfort of his concubines and catamites. He had by all accounts an interesting time, 'defiling every part of his body in dealings with persons of either sex'.

One part of his body that may have been involved here was his groin, which was disfigured by a conspicuous growth. The growth could be seen through his silken clothing, and was the subject of several poems. But he was generally careful about his appearance, sprinkling gold dust on his hair and singeing it to keep it in trim because he was terrified of barbers.

He wasn't one for false modesty, either. After a few years as emperor, he got it into his head that he was really the god Hercules, and took to parading round the streets of Rome wearing a lion skin and brandishing a club. He even had the senate deify him while he was still alive; though he might have learned from Caligula that that wasn't such a good idea.

Not content with being a living god, Commodus took on twelve official titles, so he could have the months renamed after them: Amazonius, Invictus, Felix, Pius, Lucius, Aelius, Aurelius, Commodus, Augustus, Herculeus, Romanus, Exsuperatorius. And finally, when Rome was devastated by fire in 191, he thought he would 'refound' it as 'Colonia Commodiana'.

All this was going a bit far for ordinary Romans. But Commodus had only just begun. He wanted to do something really memorable, and hit on the idea that the best way to usher

in the New Year 193 would be to stage a grand appearance in the amphitheatre dressed as a gladiator. But he also wanted to be consul, and here there was a tiny snag. In Rome, two new consuls took up office each year on January 1st; but the consuls for 193 had already been chosen. Commodus naturally decided to have both of them killed.

So it was that on 31 December 192 he went to spend the night at the school for gladiators near the Colosseum, and get ready for his big day on the morrow. But by this time he had frightened everybody so much that even his closest friends wanted rid of him. The solution was cooked up by Laetus, commander of the palace guard, and Eclectus, head of the imperial household. By accident they discovered that they too were marked down for death.

The scheme was to get Commodus's favourite concubine, Marcia, to put poison in his wine. When he came from the bath he took the poison from his lover and knocked it back in one go. It made him feel sleepy, but he had had a busy day with the animals, and nobody thought anything of it when he slipped into unconsciousness. As the poison began to act, however, Commodus came round, feeling dizzy and unwell. Then he began to be violently sick, realized what had happened, and turned very nasty. The conspirators quickly gave Narcissus his brief moment of glory. In return for a large reward, the 'strong young athlete' burst in upon the Emperor and strangled him.

CARACALLA

AD · CCXVII

Caracalla was named after a type of cloak which he particularly admired. Unfortunately, he himself was not especially admirable. He began his reign by murdering his younger brother Geta, who had been made joint-emperor with him by their father, the redoubtable Septimius Severus. Maybe his brother was insufferable, as many are; maybe Rome wasn't big enough for the two of them. But the fallout from this fratricide remained with Caracalla for the rest of his reign. Once he had killed his brother, it was easy to believe (and some later writers did) that he had threatened to kill his father and later went on to marry his mother.

Caracalla's cruellest act was at Alexandria. He stayed there during the winter of 215/216, while he was planning a war against the Parthians, but somehow the people of Alexandria upset him. Maybe they made gibes about brotherly love. Caracalla's response was simple. He called an assembly of the young men of the city, proclaiming he was going to set up a special regiment of Alexandrians (just as he had a regiment of Macedonians a couple of years earlier). When they were all gathered together,

he let his soldiers loose on them. Alexandria was the largest city of the Roman empire after Rome itself, and thousands of Alexandrians died in the ensuing massacre.

After that, Caracalla himself didn't have much longer to go. He launched his promised Parthian campaign the following summer, and caught the enemy on the hop. After much raiding and pillaging beyond the Tigris (which was the frontier at that time) Caracalla withdrew to Edessa for the winter. The plan was to renew the war the next year. So the emperor spent a pleasant winter in Edessa, while the Parthians mustered a huge army and contemplated their revenge.

When spring came, Caracalla set out from Edessa to Carrhae, the next city along, with only a small bodyguard of cavalry. He wasn't feeling too well, and eventually had to stop in order to relieve himself. So he got down from his horse and his guards turned their backs and walked a little way in the other direction, to give the emperor some privacy. All except a certain Martialis, who was quietly fuming because his brother had been executed by Caracalla a few days earlier. When he saw Caracalla alone (save for a single attendant) and the guards all looking the other way he moved forward, as if the emperor had called him over. The emperor had other things on his mind, however, and was in the process of lowering his nether garments when Martialis came behind his back and stabbed him below the shoulder-blade.

The blow was fatal and Caracalla was no more. Martialis meanwhile had run to his horse and galloped off, but he was pursued by the other guards and brought down with a well-aimed javelin.

HELIOGABALUS
AD · CCXXII

Heliogabalus is one of those emperors who was brought up with one name (a perfectly respectable Roman-sounding one) and then changed it for something else. His parents called him Varius Avitus, after his father Varius Marcellus and his uncle Julius Avitus. He changed that in his teens to Marcus Aurelius Antoninus. Then he became so devoted to a black stone that everyone began to call him Elagabalus (or Heliogabalus) after it. It was a round-topped stone, said to represent the sun god, and was kept in a temple at Emesa (modern Homs) in Syria. Why it was so sacred we don't know.

Now Marcus Aurelius Antoninus was a good name to choose at the time because Heliogabalus was trying to become emperor. To do this he pretended to be the bastard son of Caracalla. As we have seen, the emperor Caracalla was not the sort of dinner guest many people would relish, but he was popular with the army; until, at least, he was murdered. The soldiers were tickled by the idea of having his bastard son as emperor and soon overthrew the current occupant and installed Heliogabalus at Rome in his place.

Where Heliogabalus went, the black stone went with him. As High Priest of his stone, he built it a magnificent temple on the Palatine as well as a holiday villa in the suburbs. He greeted the stone every morning with strange chants, circumcised his friends, and cut open children to examine their entrails. Or so it was said. Your average Roman had no idea what all this was about, but they didn't like the dressing up in effeminate silks and satins, and they certainly didn't like the sexual antics. Maybe Heliogabalus did roam the brothels by night selling himself as a male prostitute. More likely he didn't. But his dancing and make-up didn't endear him to the palace guard.

His one great fan was his mother, Julia Soaemias. While Heliogabalus disported himself, she ruled Rome along with his grandmother Julia Maesa. But in 221 the two ladies fell out, and grandmother decided that her other grandson, Alexander Severus, would make a better emperor. Naturally, Heliogabalus and his mother didn't take too kindly to this, and tried to do away with Alexander. When that failed, he gave out that Alexander was ill and on the point of death. The soldiers didn't think much to that, either, and refused to guard Heliogabalus any longer, until Alexander was brought to their camp and shown to them.

So it was that Heliogabalus, his mother, and Alexander Severus made their way to the praetorian camp. The soldiers gave Alexander a rousing welcome and whisked him away to safety, but they cold-shouldered Heliogabalus. Roman emperors didn't take kindly to that sort of treatment, and he spent the whole night in the camp raging and fuming at the guards. Not a wise move, considering he was surrounded by nine thousand disgruntled and well-armed men.

By the next morning the soldiers had become well fed up with the tirade, and things turned nasty. Heliogabalus wanted a bloodbath of his opponents, but got one for himself instead. There are two versions of his end. In one story, when he realized his plight he hid in a chest so that he could be carried secretly to safety. Hardly a method calculated to allay suspicion; and not surprising that he was discovered by the guards and killed, at the tender age of eighteen. In the other version Heliogabalus went to hide in a privy, but the soldiers were nothing if not thorough in their rebellion, and soon pulled him out and did him in. His mother was done away with at the same time, for the sake of tidiness. In a final touching scene they had clung to one another as they were slain, and together the bodies were dragged through the streets of Rome, suffering 'desecration' and 'mutilation' on the way.

ALEXANDER SEVERUS

AD · CCXXXV

No one would call Alexander Severus one of the great emperors of Ancient Rome. Nor, on the other hand, was he one of the most evil. His claims to fame, indeed, are comparatively slight, but his death was tragic even though he himself was tiresome.

He was only thirteen when he became emperor and only twenty-six when he died. He was appointed by his grandmother to replace his unsatisfactory black-stone-worshipping cousin Heliogabalus, and didn't begin to reign until Heliogabalus had been tracked down in his privy and murdered by the praetorian guard. Even then Alexander didn't really begin to rule, since it was his mother and grandmother who really ran the government.

His feebleness eventually led to his murder. In the ninth year of Alexander's reign the Persians (who had recently taken over from the Parthians) declared war on Rome and attacked the border provinces. The emperor had no option but to go east at

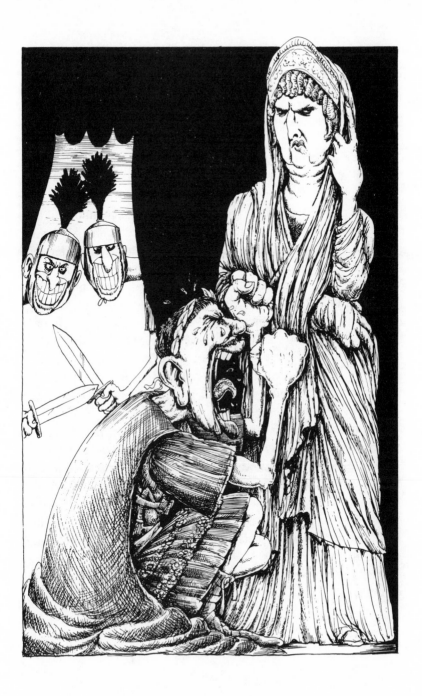

the head of a large army and stage a counter-attack. This was to be a three-pronged affair, but the main body of troops which Alexander commanded had barely crossed the frontier when he brought it to a halt. He was no warrior-king, and the Persians had little difficulty disposing of his other columns. But they stopped attacking Roman territory, and Alexander was able to disperse his army and return to the comforts of Rome.

Hardly had he got back there when there was another military emergency, this time on the Rhine. So once again Alexander found himself in the uncongenial role of field commander, this time fighting the Germans. Or that is what he should have been doing. Instead, he decided that the best thing was to buy off the enemy, trading gold for peace.

This was just too much for the soldiers, who now felt their honour was at stake. So they called on one of their commanders, Maximinus the Thracian (a career officer), and made him emperor instead. Maximinus was stationed at Mainz, training the new recruits, while Alexander and his mother were with the main army a few miles away.

At first Alexander's soldiers stood firmly behind him, but when Maximinus's recruits came into sight at dawn the next day Alexander's army refused to fight against them. Maximinus's men eventually drew near to the camp and called on the occupants to abandon the 'mean little sissy' who was still tied to his mother's apron strings. They didn't take much persuading, and Maximinus the Thracian was soon hailed as emperor by the whole army.

Alexander Severus fled back to his tent where his mother and a few friends were gathered awaiting the worst. Tearfully, the emperor clung to his mother, telling her it was her fault that everything had gone wrong. They were still doing this when the soldiers came and killed them.

None of the three Gordians died what could be called a happy death. They were easterners by origin, taking their name from Gordium, the city in Asia Minor where Alexander the Great had sliced through the Gordian knot five hundred years before. But that didn't stop them becoming key players in the Roman power game, only they didn't play it very well.

The first to come to prominence was Gordian I, who in 238 was acting as governor of the province known as Africa Proconsularis (roughly equivalent to modern Tunisia). Rome was then ruled by Maximinus the Thracian who, for all his undoubted qualities, was not popular with the Roman senate.

But at the end of the day it wasn't the senate but the people of Africa Proconsularis who first tried to unseat Maximinus. In January 238 the emperor's officials were busy collecting taxes in Thysdrus, the centre of a vast olive grove. To encourage the locals they hit upon the scheme of prosecuting the leading citizens for fictitious offences and extracting fines and confiscations. This way they could both satisfy the emperor and make a tidy profit.

If they expected the young men simply to cough up the readies, however, they were mistaken, and instead of taxes they raised a riot. The tax-gatherer-in-chief was done to death, together with his guards, and the murderers called upon Gordian to become their emperor.

Now Gordian was no spring chicken, but a man of around eighty. He had been a keen poet in his younger days, and the author of a thirty-book eulogy of the Antonine emperors, but by then was keener on sleeping than on writing. He was just settling down for a nap when the people broke in upon him and put the purple cloak around his shoulders. He hesitated to accept the office – but not for long. Though he did insist that his son, the forty-year-old Gordian II, was made joint-emperor so that he didn't have to govern on his own.

At first everything went swimmingly. The Gordians went in grand procession back to Carthage, the capital of their province, and wrote secret letters to the senate telling of their elevation. Maximinus the Thracian was away fighting Germans at the time, and the senators grasped eagerly at the opportunity to have an urbane and civilized man as their ruler. So they passed a decree making Maximinus a public enemy and acclaiming Gordian emperor.

Now all this was fine in principle, but paid scant attention to the realities of the situation, viz.:

a) that Gordian was governor of a province without any soldiers

b) that Maximinus was in command of an army of thirty thousand highly trained men

c) that Gordian had fallen out with his neighbour

Capellianus, governor of Numidia, who had six thousand soldiers of his own and was marching against Carthage at this very moment.

The Gordians tried to raise their own army but there was really little they could do to stop Capellianus. The Numidian cavalry soon overran Gordian's mob and the crack infantry of the Third Legion fought their way into Carthage. Gordian II died fighting at the barricades; Gordian I took off his belt and hanged himself.

That would have been that, had there not been yet another Gordian back in Rome. This was Gordian III, grandson of Gordian I and nephew of Gordian II. When the first two Gordians were killed the crowds at Rome demanded that Gordian III should be made co-emperor with Pupienus and Balbinus, though he was only thirteen. Within three months Maximinus, Pupienus, and Balbinus had all been murdered, which left Gordian sole ruler by default.

Gordian III was obviously too young to reign without advisers, and here he was lucky: a man called Gaius Furius Sabinus Aquila Timesitheus did most of the work, and did it conscientiously and efficiently. Gordian even married his daughter. For five years all went well, until in 243 Timesitheus decided on a Persian campaign. The campaign was a success, and the Persians were steadily pushed back, but Timesitheus fell ill and died, deep within enemy territory.

His protector gone, Gordian III soon fell victim to the wiles of an Arab called Philip, who became the new commander-in-chief. He cunningly disrupted the food supplies and laid the blame on Gordian, saying he was too young to rule. The soldiers naturally believed every word. Gordian, young though he was, was outraged by this slander, and climbed on to a platform to tell the assembled the army the real reason for the shortages of food and drink. The soldiers wouldn't listen. So he asked them bluntly which they would prefer as emperor, Philip or himself. Not a smart move; inevitably Gordian lost. He was carried out of sight, kicking and screaming, and done away with.

PUPIENUS AND BALBINUS

AD · CCXXXVIII

Few Roman emperors were more obscure (or more short-lived) than Pupienus and Balbinus. This elderly pair were appointed by the senate when news came that Gordians I and II had been killed at Carthage. They set about organizing resistance to Maximinus the Thracian, who was the real Roman emperor at the time, and who was marching on Italy to exact a terrible vengeance on his opponents.

In the event, Maximinus got no further than Aquileia, at the head of the Adriatic. He was busy besieging the city when some of his soldiers (tired of fighting their fellow-citizens) burst into his tent and murdered him. Pupienus and Balbinus were naturally delighted. They disbanded the army and returned to Rome with only the praetorian guard and a special detachment of Germans of whom Pupienus was particularly fond.

Back in the capital they soon started to squabble over which of them was the more important. Balbinus thought he was the more distinguished of the two, but it was Pupienus who had the

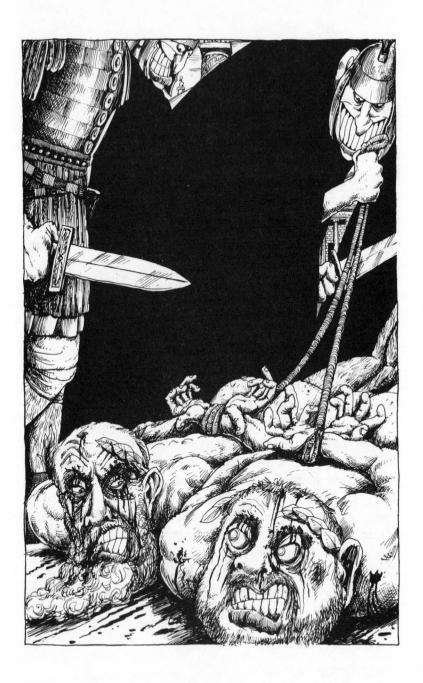

all-important military background. The praetorian guard didn't wait for them to decide. They had murdered Maximinus not for love of Pupienus and Balbinus but for a quiet ife. So now they murdered Pupienus and Balbinus as well. They reckoned that Gordian III, a young lad of thirteen, was much less likely to cause trouble, and made him sole emperor instead.

VALERIAN

AD · CCLX

Valerian is one of the obvious candidates for most unfortunate Roman emperor, with Trebonianus Gallus (251–253) a close second. Their great enemy was Shapur I, the cruel and wicked (though rather successful) king of Persia. It was Shapur who had attacked the Roman empire in the time of Gordian III, and had been bought off with huge bribes by Philip the Arab. But Shapur wasn't a once-in-a-lifetime kind of man, and felt that one success deserved another. He therefore sat back and waited for the next opportunity to devastate the Roman empire. And if that didn't work, he could always hope for another handsome pay-off.

The right moment came when the Roman legions decided, as so often in these years, to have a spell fighting each other rather than any foreign enemy. The catalogue of disasters begins in 251, when the emperor Decius was chasing the Goths (a violent Germanic people) out of the Balkans where they had spent some months raiding the Roman provinces. Decius had the upper hand, but then threw it all away by marching his army into a trap in which both he and they perished. It was the first time a Roman emperor had been killed by a foreign enemy.

His place was taken by the euphoniously named Trebonianus Gallus (or Imperator Caesar Gaius Vibius Trebonianus Gallus Piux Felix Invictus Augustus, to give him his full name; though the Felix, or 'Fortunate', was not borne out by events). He began by paying the Goths to go away (a short-sighted move), and then travelled to Rome. Here he spent his time dealing with a major outbreak of plague. Next came news that Shapur I had crossed the frontier and launched his second attack on the eastern provinces. Then Gallus heard that the Goths had broken their peace treaty and crossed into the Balkans again. Soon afterwards a message arrived saying that they had been defeated by the local Roman commander Aemilianus. Good news indeed; but closely followed by word that that commander had now decided to become emperor himself and was at that very moment marching on Rome.

Gallus was taken unawares and killed by his own soldiers as soon as his rival drew near with his army. It was at this point that Valerian makes his appearance on the page of history. He was off raising new troops in the Balkans when Gallus was killed, and at once decided that he too would have a go at becoming emperor. So he marched on Rome, and this time it was Aemilianus who was murdered as Valerian approached.

Valerian chased Shapur out of Syria and spent several years on the eastern frontier, getting his own back against the Persians. He was doing rather well, when in 260 Shapur decided he had had enough and launched a massive counter-attack. It was then that Valerian suffered the singular misfortune of having his army struck down by plague. They holed up in the city of Edessa, hoping to escape from the Persians, but Shapur followed them and besieged them. Soon it was not only disease but shortage of water they had to contend with. The soldiers began to look mutinous, and Valerian decided he had no option but to do a deal with the Persians. Together with a small entourage he rode out of Edessa and went to talk to Shapur. That would have been fine if Shapur had been a man of honour. Only he wasn't. He didn't waste words on Valerian, but simply sent him back a prisoner to Persia.

In later years, Roman historians of the Christian persuasion thought this was a Good Thing. It showed that emperors like Valerian who persecuted the Christians came to a sticky end. Small wonder that Valerian had wanted to persecute them.

Valerian's end is shrouded in mystery, but one thing is sure – it was ignominious. Shapur used him as a human mounting-block whenever he got on or off his horse. When eventually Valerian died, his skin was flayed from the body, dyed with vermilion, and hung in a Persian temple. From that time on, whenever Roman ambassadors came to Persia they were shown the skin of Valerian to remind them of their disgrace.

POSTUMUS
AD · CCLXIX

Postumus was the world's first famous Belgian. His people, the Batavians, lived around the mouth of the Rhine, and provided fierce cavalrymen for the Roman army. There was even a Batavian cavalry squadron on Hadrian's Wall.

We know very little about Postumus himself, which is a pity, because he was an enterprising individual who decided to set up an empire of his own. This he did by carving off the western provinces of the Roman empire (while the Romans were busy elsewhere fighting Goths and Persians), and making himself emperor over Britain, Gaul, the Rhineland, and Spain. It was a bold scheme, and it worked. For almost ten years, from 260 to 269, Postumus governed his so-called Gallic empire, proclaiming himself 'Imperator' and 'Augustus' and all the usual titles.

The real Roman emperor, Gallienus, did have one go at getting rid of Postumus. He led his army across the Alps into Gaul, but then was wounded during a siege and decided he had had enough.

Postumus made Trier his capital and was staying there towards the end of 268 when he heard that one of his command-

ers had done to him what he had done to Gallienus, i.e., revolted. The villain was one Laelianus, governor of Upper Germany. Postumus mustered his troops and marched against Laelianus, defeating him early in 269 just outside Mainz. Now Mainz was Laelianus's capital, and Postumus's troops thought this an excellent opportunity for a bit of plunder and pillaging. Postumus was a man who took his duties seriously, however, and would not have his troops slaughtering what were his own subjects. So he refused, and Mainz survived. Only Postumus didn't. Because he wouldn't allow them to sack the city, his soldiers killed him.

CARUS & CO.

AD · CCLXXXIII, CCLXXXIV, AND CCLXXXV

Of all Roman emperors, Carus probably had the most original death. Stabbings, poisonings, and suicides are commonplace enough, but to be struck by a bolt of lightning is rather a surprise. No one was more surprised than Carus. He was a good man, by some accounts – which isn't usually the recipe for an interesting life. But whatever his failings, he redeemed them all by expiring, literally, in a blaze of glory.

At the time he was busy with the conquest of Persia, that occasional pastime of all Roman emperors. In fact he'd just captured their capital city and was in his tent on the banks of the River Tigris when the disaster occurred. 'There suddenly arose a storm of such violence that all things grew black and none could recognize another; then continuous flashes of lightning and peals of thunder, like bolts from a fiery sky, took from us all the power of knowing what truly befell.' The poor man could hardly have known what hit him. Unless, that is, the lightning came in human form, with a dagger in one hand and a firebrand in the other.

Now Carus had taken his son with him to the east, a sickly feeble teenager called Numerian. He was especially good at poetry, for what that was worth, but his end was neither poetic nor epic. He was already ill when the untimely lightning fried his father. The illness affected his eyes and blinded him, so he was carried all the way from the River Tigris in a closed litter. Someone soon decided he would be better dead as well. Not in itself a surprising turn of events. What was unusual was that the author of this dark deed decided to pretend Numerian was still alive. Several days went by before the soldiers realized that what they were carrying across Turkey was not an emperor but a corpse. It was the stench of putrefaction which eventually gave the game away.

The murderer was never caught, but the soldiers were easily persuaded to kill Numerian's father-in-law as a likely culprit. They then elected Diocletian, one of their own commanders, as emperor. This was hardly calculated to amuse Numerian's brother Carinus, who was emperor in the west. Indeed, Carinus was not a very amusing man. He may have smiled as he deflowered young maidens, and his musical tastes extended to singers and pantomimes, but that (according to our sources) was about as far as it went. He had other curious tastes; for 'swimming' in apples and melons, and bathing in specially cooled water. If the water was even slightly warm his attendants were given an earful and accused of treating him like a woman. You can almost feel sorry for him, though not for long.

It was his interest in other men's wives that proved his undoing. Carinus fought a great battle against Diocletian in the Balkans, but when things began to go his way his officers became

appalled at the idea that he might win. He had been hard enough to take when he was only a half-emperor; what would he be like on his own? And how would they keep his hands off their wives? There was only one solution; to do him in in the thick of the fighting. Like a corpse in a cemetery, a killing in a battle doesn't attract much attention.

It is not recorded whether the assassins escaped unscathed, but they'd have won a sincere vote of thanks from Carinus' old classmates; any, that is, who'd survived. For one of his nastier traits was to hunt down the boys who had laughed at him at school and exact revenge. Perhaps he had been bullied as a lad.

In general, Roman emperors were parted from power only by death. They enjoyed being in control, and only gave up when they had to. If they were forced to abdicate, as some of the last emperors were, then it was an act not of their choosing. These men were nothing if not ambitious. Or frightened. For how could they be sure their successors would leave them to live out their old age in peace?

The exception to them all is Diocletian. He reigned for twenty years, put the Roman world to rights, and then retired to grow cabbages at his villa by the sea.

The secret of his success was his passion for organization. Diocletian was wise enough to realize that ruling the whole empire had become just too much for any one man. No one could be fighting Germans on the Rhine and Sarmatians on the Danube at the same time. Even less so when he was also fighting Persians in Armenia and Moors in Mauretania. The answer was simple: to have not just one emperor, but a whole college of emperors, four in number, each responsible for a different section of the frontier. It was expensive – each of the four lived in imperial style. It was also dangerous, to a degree – how could one be sure they wouldn't fight each other rather than the Germans or Sarmatians? But amazingly it worked.

Diocletian was around forty years old when he seized power from the festering corpse of Numerian in 284. The next year he became supreme ruler of the whole Roman World when Carinus was murdered. Within a few months he had appointed another man to help him – Maximian – so that Diocletian ruled the eastern provinces while Maximian ruled the west. He even gave Maximian the city of Rome, since it was no longer of much importance. Then in 293 both men appointed junior assistants to spread the load even further: Constantius in the west, Galerius in the east.

This multiplication of emperors may well have confused the common people. That was partly intentional. An emperor was an emperor, deserving taxes and respect, whatever his name. Their statues showed them looking all the same. As far as their subjects were concerned these were nameless faces of power.

The system was a great success. The other emperors did what Diocletian told them to, and fought his wars for him. He made the empire stronger than it had been for eighty years. But he was not without his faults, the most memorable being the persecution of Christians which he launched in 303. The tortures and executions were taken up with gusto by Christian writers who revelled in recording the awesomely awful deaths which God visited on the perpetrators.

In this visitation of divine justice Diocletian got off relatively lightly. But he was growing old, and late in 304, just after celebrating twenty years in power, he began to feel ill. That

didn't stop him from setting out on a long journey in the middle of winter, but he got worse and worse and at last he collapsed. Everyone thought he would die, but miraculously he recovered and decided that now was the moment to retire. Some years before he had begun to build a magnificent palace on the shore of the Adriatic, at Split. Perhaps he had intended all along to end his days there. Whatever the truth of the matter, on 1 May 305 he handed power to his junior colleague Galerius and left for the seaside.

From this point on things began to go wrong. The four emperors had worked well enough while Diocletian had been in charge. Now they began to fight among themselves. One of the main problems was Maximian, his erstwhile colleague, who had been forced to retire at the same time. Maximian couldn't bear a quiet life and began to dabble in politics again, together with his son Maxentius, who set himself up as emperor at Rome.

When things got really bad they decided to call a conference at Carnuntum on the Danube, and invited Diocletian to leave his retirement and join them. When he arrived, Maximian tried to persuade Diocletian to take up the reins of power once again. Diocletian, however, had learned the delights of peacefulness and leisure, and declared he took such delight in growing cabbages at Split that nothing could tempt him back.

Diocletian lived on for three more years, but his story didn't have the happy ending we might expect. It was all Maximian's fault. Discontented as ever, he tried to overthrow the new western emperor, Constantine, in 310. When this failed, he took refuge at Marseilles, but the people simply opened the gates and let in Constantine's men. Maximian was found conveniently hanged. His wife, Diocletian's daughter, fled to the east where she was cast into the Syrian desert by the new eastern emperor Maximinus. Diocletian's entreaties for his daughter to be returned to him fell on stony ground. The final twist came when Constantine began to destroy Maximian's statues and memorials. Most of them showed Diocletian and Maximian together, but this didn't stop Constantine from destroying them.

The shame was too much for Diocletian, who took to his bed. There he tossed about in torment, neither sleeping nor eating, but sighing, groaning, and weeping. Until at last he died. Which goes to show that cabbages alone are not enough.

GALERIUS

AD · CCCXI

The emperor Galerius was one of Diocletian's recruits, and was given the eastern half of the empire to govern when Diocletian abdicated. He was also given a junior emperor, the unpleasant Maximin Daia, to help him. The two were keen on persecuting Christians, and Christian writers were delighted to record that both died nasty deaths.

Galerius's end was particularly revolting. He had been reigning for six years when of a sudden a suppurating inflammation broke out around his genitals, followed by a terrible ulcer.

He was consumed by worms, and his body dissolved and rotted amid insupportable pain ... Cooked meats were placed near his dissolving buttocks so that the heat could draw out the worms; when these were broken up, countless numbers of the creatures swarmed around; the very disaster to his rotting flesh had proved fertile in generating an even greater quantity of them.

The doctors could do nothing; some couldn't bear the stench and were executed for their squeamishness. Others were killed

because their remedies didn't work. Meanwhile the illness continued its terrible progress:

Now that the evil had spread, the parts of his body had lost their form. The upper part of it down to the wound had dried up, and in its pitiable thinness the skin had turned sallow and sunk between his bones; the lower part had spread out like leather bags, and his feet had lost their shape. This had gone on continually for a year, when at last, subdued by his ills, he was compelled to confess God ... A few days later, with the limbs throughout his body now disintegrating, he was carried off by the dreadful wasting.

MAXIMIN DAIA

AD · CCCXIII

Maximin Daia has two claims to fame: his cruelty and his death. His cruelty we learn of mainly through the writings of the Christians he so enjoyed persecuting. His agents even forged a special book, the *Acts of Pilate*, to show how the gospels had got the story all wrong. Maximin also forced Christians to make sacrifice to the pagan gods, on pain of imprisonment and death, and where he didn't kill the culprits he mutilated them by gouging out their eyes or cutting off some part or other of their bodies (hands, feet, noses, ears ...). But it was the Christians who had the last laugh, since they were able to portray Maximin as a cruel monster (which he may not have been) and write gleeful accounts of his horrible end.

Now at the time Maximin was around the government of the Roman empire was divided between several emperors, each of whom had his own bundle of provinces. In this division of power, Maximin had control of the east, extending from Egypt through Syria and into Asia Minor. The idea was that the different emperors should work together, but in practice they spent quite a lot of time fighting or intriguing against each other.

It was this that led to Maximin's downfall. While he was gaily persecuting Christians in the east a new and more powerful emperor had emerged in the west, one furthermore who was pro-Christian: Constantine. Constantine ordered Maximin to halt his persecution (which he did), but then allied himself with Maximin's great rival, Licinius, the emperor of the Balkans. Maximin decided it was a case of kill or be killed, so he ferried his army across the Bosphorus and attacked Licinius, but in the battle which followed he was defeated.

Maximin fled the battlefield in disguise and was chased by Licinius across Asia Minor. He tried to defend the passes leading to Syria, but was defeated again and cornered in the city of Tarsus. He decided that there was nothing for it but to take his own life, but badly botched the job when he tried. Or perhaps he died of disease. But it is the suicide story which gives the more lurid end. Thinking he was eating his last meal, Maximin treated himself to a banquet before taking the poison. But he was so full it made him sick rather than killing him, and the dose which his body retained was not enough to finish him quickly.

His death agonies were awesomely gruesome, a fact the Christian writers don't fail to stress. In fact, the pain caused by the poison was so unbearable that he went mad for four days, going so far as to eat soil. Then he battered his head against a wall so that his eyes fell out of their sockets. As he lay dying in torment, he saw a vision of God and his angels passing judgement against him. Rather late in the day, he decided that persecuting the Christians had perhaps been a bad move. He certainly never did it again.

JULIAN

AD · CCCLXIII

The emperor Julian rejoices in the name 'the Apostate', because he rejected Christianity and returned to the worship of the old gods of Greece and Rome. He was an educated lover of classical civilization, who had been called from his studies to become junior emperor in the west. After a few years, however, he had marched against the senior emperor (Constantius II) and over-thrown him – though Constantius died before battle could be joined.

Christianity had become the state religion of the Roman empire almost fifty years before under Constantine. Paganism was far from dead, but Christians enjoyed all the privileges including tax exemptions and imperial patronage for the building of churches. Julian thought this was all wrong. He saw Christi-anity as the enemy of the classical values he so loved. But he wanted not to outlaw Christianity, simply to put it on a more even footing with other religions. So he took away its privileges and encouraged the building of temples instead. He was also rather keen on sacrifices, of any and every kind, to an extent that disgusted even many ardent pagans. One writer says that if

Julian had survived his Persian campaign the Roman world would soon have experienced a cattle shortage.

The Persian campaign was the big event of the reign. Constantius II had already fallen out with his eastern neighbours, who were attacking the Roman frontier regions. After Constantius's death it fell to Julian to take the necessary action.

Julian was not a modest man. He thought he was destined to be the new Alexander the Great, conqueror of Persia. Others had thought so before, and none had come very well out of it. Julian went even further – he thought he was Alexander's reincarnation. And in keeping with his belief in the old gods he did what every good pagan ruler should do: before setting out on campaign he sent emissaries to consult the oracles. The reply came in typically cryptic form: 'We the gods are starting out to carry off the trophies of victory by the bestial river; I, Ares, raising the din of war, am leading them!' The 'bestial river' was the Tigris (= tiger, a beast). Ares was the Greek god of war. Everything seemed set for victory.

At first, the expedition went well. Julian's army sailed down the River Euphrates in a flotilla of over a thousand ships, until they drew parallel to Ctesiphon, the Persian capital. Now Ctesiphon is not on the Euphrates but on the Tigris, and in order to attack Ctesiphon Julian had to clear out an old canal which ran between the two rivers. Having done so and beaten off a Persian attack he encamped his army in front of the city and began to besiege it.

At this point things began to go wrong. The Romans were deep in the heart of enemy territory, in a landscape crisscrossed by irrigation canals, with enemy forces all around them, making it very difficult to gather food and other supplies. Provisions began to run low, the city was strongly defended, and Julian looked about for another way of winning the war.

So he decided to leave Ctesiphon and move westwards again. But rather than sailing back up the Euphrates (perhaps because the current would have been against them), he burned almost all his ships and withdrew by land. Here Julian had the bad luck or poor judgement to rely on local informers who were in reality Persian spies. Instead of leading the Romans through fertile lands as they had promised, they led them into a wilderness where the army was even worse off than it had been before. The Persians had beaten them to it, and burned or carried off crops and cattle. It was a highly effective scorched earth policy.

As if shortages and summer heat (it was now June) were not enough, the Persians harried the Romans all the way. Julian was encouraging his troops in the midst of one of these skirmishes when fate intervened. There was a commotion, a Persian attack, and the emperor was hit by a javelin which pierced his side near the groin.

Nobody was sure who had done it. The obvious culprits were the Persians themselves, but some thought it was one of Julian's own side who was responsible, perhaps some disaffected Christian or a soldier enraged by Julian's incompetent conduct of the campaign.

The last pagan emperor fell mortally wounded, and was carried from the battlefield on a shield. Relying on Ares had done him no good at all. He recognized his own downfall, and cast his hand in the air, scattering his blood and crying, 'Take your fill, Nazarene!' The new gods had won.

HONORIUS, VALENTINIAN, AND GLYCERIUS THE BISHOP

If ever there were a competition for worst Roman emperor (not wickedest, simply worst) then Honorius would be worth a hefty wager. It wasn't only that he sat tight in Ravenna while the Goths sacked Rome. He also lost most of the western provinces: Britain, Gaul, the Rhineland, and Spain. In fact, once he was finished, there was very little left. Maybe it wasn't entirely his fault, but nobody could make it out to have been a successful reign.

His son Valentinian would come a close second.

Honorius was hardly an impressive figure in any sense. He was only ten years old when he became emperor, and didn't improve much in later life. He was said to have neither passions, nor talents, nor energy for anything. Yet he reigned

longer than any of his immediate predecessors, a reign of almost thirty years.

By this time the Roman empire had been divided into two parts, the eastern half ruled from Constantinople, the western half from Ravenna. The eastern half survived as the Byzantine empire, falling only to the Ottoman Turks in 1453. Honorius, Valentinian, and their successors ruled only the western part of the original empire. And didn't make a very good job of it either.

The most notable event of Honorius's years in power was his failure to defend Rome against Alaric and the Visigoths. Alaric had spent some time causing trouble and distress in the Balkans but in 407 shifted his sights to Italy. There followed a great toing and froing of armies and ambassadors, as Honorius and his advisers tried to persuade Alaric to go home and leave them alone, while Alaric tried to extort a good price for his compliance. They had almost reached agreement when Alaric ran out of patience and put the eternal city to fire and the sword, Gothic style.

Fortunately for Honorius, Alaric died soon after sacking Rome.

Honorius's death, when it came, was remarkably undramatic. Having put down a few rivals and lost some more territory he died of dropsy in August 423, aged thirty-nine.

Unfortunately his son Valentinian III was on hand to carry on the family tradition. First of all, he too was a mere child when he came to power – only six years old. Once again he left affairs of state to his ministers and womenfolk. Second, he too quickly lost large chunks of the empire: notably North Africa, which was captured by the Vandals. And thirdly, he reigned a long time, but nobody (apart from himself) derived much benefit from the fact.

The great excitement of the reign was the invasion of Attila the Hun. It was all the fault of Valentinian's sister, Honoria. Valentinian wanted her to marry, but she didn't like the man he had chosen for her. So she wrote to Attila (who had been attacking the Balkans) and sent him her ring. Attila knew a good thing when he saw one, and at once demanded Honoria for his wife and half the western empire as her dowry. Valentinian refused, and Attila promptly invaded Gaul.

The Huns were a redoubtable lot, and for a moment it must have seemed that nothing could stop them. But Valentinian was saved by an astute general called Aetius, who managed to persuade all the warring factions – Romans, Gauls, and Germans – that Attila the Hun was not in their best interest. In 451 a great battle was fought at the Catalaunian Fields in northern Gaul, and Attila was forced to withdraw.

Attila died two years later. But Valentinian was not yet out of the wood by any means, since he now had to face his overmighty general Aetius. The latter demanded that his son marry the emperor's oldest daughter Eudocia (then at the advanced age of twelve). Valentinian prevaricated, lured Aetius to the imperial palace at Rome, and had him killed.

It wasn't a bright move. For a start, although Aetius was powerful, he at least had shown he could defend the empire (what was left of it). As one contemporary said to Valentinian: 'I don't know what your trouble was, but you seem to have cut off your right hand with your left.'

Valentinian didn't survive long enough to test the moral. He was processing on his way to the races in March 455 when two army officers still loyal to Aetius took their revenge by cutting his throat.

The emperors who followed were easily disposed of. For one thing, each of them reigned only a few months. For another, they had very little control of events. That was now in the hands of the barbarian (German) officers who commanded the army, men such as Ricimer the Suevian, Gundobad the Burgundian, and Odoacer the Scirian (or was he a Goth?).

In point of fact, nine emperors ruled Rome from the death of Valentinian III in 455 to the end of the line twenty-one years later. That gave them an average of two years' reign apiece, though in fact one ruled as long as five years and most of them much less. Only two of them died peacefully in office. Four came to violent ends, while the other three were got rid of in various non-violent ways.

One of the more ingenious non-violent disposals was that visited on Glycerius. His predecessor Olybrius had reigned only seven months before inconsiderately dying of dropsy. This gave Gundobad (who was chief barbarian at the time) the trouble of choosing a replacement. He waited for four months before making up his mind, then appointed Flavius Glycerius, who thus became last-but-second emperor of Rome.

Glycerius assumed the purple in March 473 and was forced to abandon it a year later. The problem for him was that the eastern emperor (based at Constantinople) liked neither him nor his barbarian backers and sent an army to remove him. Glycerius fled to Rome but the people shut the city gates against him and he was captured at Portus nearby. Rather than kill him, the commander of the eastern invaders, one Julius Nepos, showed some imagination and made him a priest. No clergyman could possibly reign as emperor. So Glycerius ended his days as the Bishop of Salonae on the Dalmatian coast.

ROMULUS
THE LAST
AD · CCCLXXVI

By a strange quirk of fate the last emperor of Rome was called Romulus. He came to power through the good offices of his father Orestes (who had once held the unlikely position of secretary to Attila the Hun). Like previous emperors Romulus took the title Augustus, but since he was only fourteen years old people called him Augustulus, 'the little Augustus', instead.

He reigned for only eleven months. In the summer of 476 the army in Italy (now comprised mainly of barbarians) rose in revolt and claimed a third of the country for themselves. Orestes refused and was decapitated for his stubbornness. The more pliable Romulus showed a wisdom far beyond his years. He was captured at Ravenna in September 476, and willingly wrote a letter of abdication to the senate. Odoacer, commander of the German levies, became the king of Italy (there were to be no more emperors) and sent Romulus Augustulus with an annual pension of six thousand gold pieces to live out the rest of his life in comfortable retirement on the Bay of Naples. Which of us wouldn't have done the same?

EPITAPH

The emperor Domitian used to say that the lot of princes was most unhappy, since when they discovered a conspiracy no one believed them unless they had been killed. He was slain on the fourteenth day before the Kalends of October in the forty-fifth year of his age and the fifteenth of his reign.